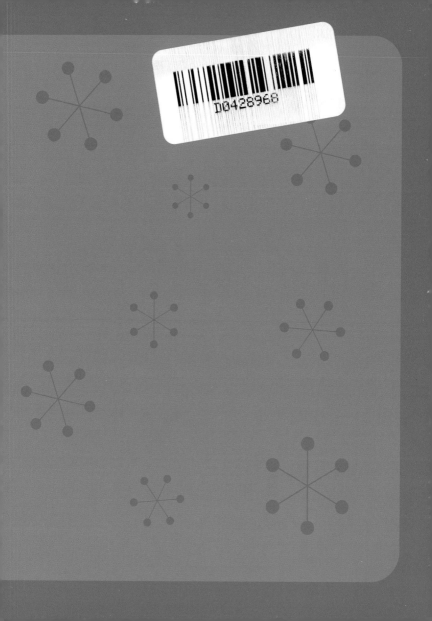

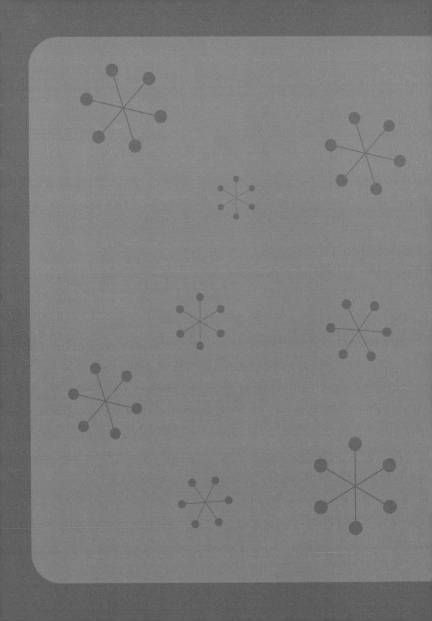

Dig your way to a
FABULOUS LIFE

LAGOON
BOOKS

Project Editor: Sylvia Goulding
Book Design: Norma Martin

Thanks to: Ann Marangos, Nick Daws, Claire Redhead,
Jeremy Hemming and Geeta Narayanan

Cover Design: River Design
Illustrations: Gary Sherwood

Series Editor: Lucy Dear
Managing Editor: Sarah Wells
Based on an original concept by Simon Melhuish

Published by:
LAGOON BOOKS
PO BOX 311, KT2 5QW, UK
PO BOX 990676, Boston, MA 02199 USA

ISBN: 1902813766

Printed in Thailand

This book has been written to apply to most temperate climate zones. If you live in an
extremely cold or hot zone, please check with your garden center or nursery.

Dig your way to a

FABULOUS LIFE

Introduction

Whether you have a large or a tiny patch, your garden will be the answer to all your hopes and dreams — a fabulous life is guaranteed if you just dig in...

Clever Tips
Become the envy of all your friends and neighbors - and add a touch of magic to your own life.

Hi there! Is life failing to deliver on its promises to you? Never mind! In the words of the old Chinese proverb, "He who plants a garden, plants happiness." Wonderful, magical things happen in gardens — just ask Adam and Eve!

In a beautiful garden you, and your life, really can be transformed. In this book you'll learn how to turn your plot into an earthly paradise with little more than a wave of your 'magic' shovel. Here are just some of the wonders awaiting you in the green pages that follow...

Lazy Gardening

Good news! Gardening doesn't have to be hard work. In this chapter you'll learn how you can stop doing those chores you hate. Give up weeding with *Out of the Limelight*, give up mowing with *Mostly Moss*. Once you've stopped doing all those tedious tasks, you'll start to see your garden as the place it should be – a haven of relaxation and delight.

Year Round Color the Easy Way

Bright, beautiful colors lift everyone's spirits. In this chapter you'll learn how to ensure your garden remains a riot of color, even in the darkest days of winter. Plant a display of life-enriching golden yellow flowers in *Bring Me Sunshine*, or a glorious *Tub of Hope* to herald the start of the spring. Can't you feel your life getting better even now?

Party Time
Get your garden ready with lights, BBQ, and the food to serve, for the best party in the world.

Fabulous Outdoor Living

We all need fresh air to put color in our cheeks and a song in our hearts. In this chapter you'll learn easy techniques to transform even the smallest garden into a vibrant, revitalizing living area. *Light up your life* with well-chosen outdoor lights and candles, then turn your patch into a *Stairway to heaven* with a simple trick from southern France, and transform your lawn into a scented paradise with a *Bop-till-you-drop garden.*

The Good Life

Gardens aren't just to be admired but to be consumed with all the senses. Find out in this chapter how to grow your own tasty herbs and vegetables, ready to enjoy in an *al fresco* feast. In *Club Med* you'll discover how to evoke the flavor of the Mediterranean in your garden, while in *Table setting* you'll create a fairy-tale outdoor dining table which magically replenishes itself!

It's true! A beautiful garden has the power to transform the lives of those lucky enough to own one. Follow the advice in this book, and as your garden grows, your life will grow and blossom with it. Romance, happiness, wealth, peace of mind, success — whatever you most want from living, a beautiful garden can be your key to achieving it. So why wait any longer? Turn the page, and start digging. Your fabulous life awaits!

LAZY GARDENING

YEAR ROUND COLOR THE EASY WAY

FABULOUS OUTDOOR LIVING

THE GOOD LIFE

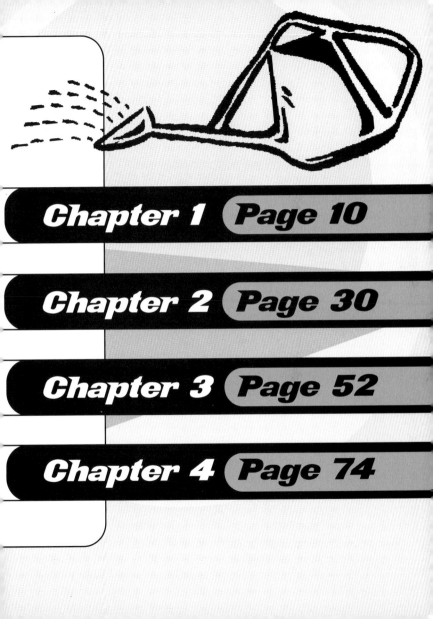

LAZY GARDENING

Chapter One

MAKE YOUR GARDEN LOOK AFTER ITSELF,
LEAVING YOU FREE TO ENJOY LIFE!

Out of the limelight

Does your garden look less than fabulous because it's overrun with weeds? Don't allow them to tyrannize you. Follow the easy way to a weed-free patch.

Water savers

There are two other important advantages to using ground-cover plants: they are environment friendly because they require much less water and fertilizer than a lawn, and the plants also provide a visually pleasing green link between other plants, for example between clumps of flowers and trees or flowering shrubs.

Weeds need air, light, and water. One easy way to keep those pesky weeds out of your garden is to deprive them of light and smother them with other, more desirable plants.

What to Choose

● Cotoneaster 'Skogholm Coral Beauty' – a spreading, groundcovering variety; particularly good on sloping ground

● Cranesbill (*Geranium endressii* 'Wargrave Pink') – an attractive, fast-spreading, pink-flowered, perennial geranium; good in full sun

● Persian ivy (*Hedera colchica*) – large, dark green leaves; perfect for shade

● Juniper (*Juniperus communis* 'Depressa Aurea') – with golden foliage in summer if planted in a sunny spot; good on sloping ground

● Groundcover roses – *Rosa* 'Red Dagmar' (reddish purple flowers with attractive hips in autumn [fall]); *R.* 'Magic Carpet' (pink, fragrant); *R.* 'Euphoria' (orange-yellow, fragrant); particularly good in full sun

● Saxifrage – many varieties, spreading groundcover with dainty little flowers.

How to Do it

1. Thoroughly weed (just the once!) the ground and dig over, removing as many roots as you can.
2. Plant your chosen groundcover plants, at the distances suggested on the labels; water in by giving them plenty of water.
3. For the first year, carefully weed between plants until they have become established and started spreading. Eventually they will join up and leave no spot of ground uncovered.

Aftercare

Your groundcover plants will need no special aftercare. Simply cut out any dead parts, and cut back around the edges if they start spreading beyond their allotted area. Lie back and read a book while leaving the garden to weed itself.

A WEED IS A PLANT WHOSE VIRTUES HAVE NOT YET BEEN DISCOVERED...
[RALPH WALDO EMERSON]

Smothered with love

A simple trick will help you get a stranglehold over your weeds, rather than them having you in a clinch – smother them, and enjoy lots more free party-time.

Multi-colored dream mulch

Dyes are now available from specialist DIY and garden centers and from the manufacturers, which you can pour directly into the machine while shredding wood. This allows you to produce your very own designer bark chips in a variety of colors. You can use these to create color patterns in your garden.

Simply cover the ground with a thick and weed-impenetrable "mulch", and you will suffocate even the most persistent weeds, once and for all. You can do this for as large an area of the garden as you like. Your plants will be grateful for the extra weather protection afforded by the mulch, and you get the added benefit of an attractive cover of stones or woodchips.

What to Choose

● Organic mulches – well-rotted manure, compost, leaf mold, hay, straw, bark chips, cocoa shells
● Inorganic mulches – stones, gravel; black plastic, or so-called geotextiles, or weed barriers (black or white fabric containing polypropylene or polyester which permit water and gases to pass through).

How to Do it

1. In the autumn (fall) thoroughly weed the

ground you wish to mulch, removing as many roots as possible. If you are intending to use a water-impermeable mulch such as black plastic, water the ground thoroughly before.

2. Cover the ground with the mulch. If using stones or gravel, apply a 7 ½ cm (3 in) layer. If using an organic material allow for the mulch to settle; apply 10 cm (4 in) of fine material and up to 15 cm (6 in) of coarse material such as straw.

3. Leave a 5 cm (2 in) mulch-free circle around the base of each garden plant for breathing room.

4. Re-apply a fresh layer of mulch every two or three years, when the original layer becomes worn out.

Aftercare

Single large weeds may come through an organic mulch, but they're easy to pull out. If using black plastic, make sure that your plants will not suffer during hot spells; add a layer of soil on top of the plastic to stop the ground over-heating.

I USED TO LOVE MY GARDEN BUT NOW MY LOVE IS DEAD FOR I FOUND A BACHELOR'S BUTTON IN BLACK-EYED SUSAN'S BED...*
[C P SAWYER]

* both bachelor's button and black-eyed Susan are garden plants

Repo man

If none of your efforts bear fruit, and weeds will insist on spoiling the scene, there's only one way out: re-possess your garden, and make it the envy of your friends again!

English gardens

Although garden history goes back to China and Ancient Egypt, lawns are recent inventions. They first appeared in the 17th century, in England. They were supposed to show the owner's wealth – he had money to employ staff and the leisure time to create and enjoy an unproductive area within the larger garden.

Weeds may be hard to keep under control, if the time you have to devote to your garden is limited. So turn your weed plantation into stunning outdoor seating and weed-free zones.

What to Choose

● Wooden decking – use pressure-treated timber (lumber) boards, or pre-assembled square decking tiles. Wooden decking invokes days by the seaside, bamboo paving will create an Asiatic mood

● Paved patios – use old flagstones, or old-look concrete stones, or lay pre-assembled mosaic tiles on a concrete base for a Mediterranean feel

● Gravel gardens – choose small gravel for large areas and punctuate this with a few large stones or wooden paths; choose different color pebbles for different areas, separated by borders; create a Japanese garden by raking patterns into the gravel

● Chippings – colored glass chippings are very attractive and can be laid to create patterns; wood chippings give a natural woodland effect

● Concrete – colored and textured concrete makes an easy-care and attractive patio surface.

How to Do it

1. Dig up all remaining areas of lawn. Weed the ground, remove roots and large stones.

2. Rake the ground flat, allowing for a slight fall away from the house. Firm the ground with a roller.

3. For rigid surfaces (decking, paving), add a 5–10 cm (2–4 in) layer hardcore (stones, crocks), firm with a compactor or roller. Top with a 5 cm (2 in) layer sand, and compact again. For loose surfaces (eg gravel), place a 5 cm (2 in) layer sand, compact, cover with geotextile membrane between sand and gravel.

4. Edge with railway sleepers (railroad ties), bricks, or wooden boards to stop your patio "walking".

5. Green up your patio: use plants in containers, or fill planting holes with flowers, shrubs, or climbers to add life to the garden.

TO SIT IN THE SHADE ON A FINE DAY AND LOOK UPON VERDURE IS THE MOST PERFECT REFRESHMENT...
[JANE AUSTEN]

Drought-proof garden

Banish those days of dragging a heavy watering can across the lawn – let your plants find their own drinks, and settle for the good life with a glass of champagne.

Do nothing and get paid for it

As part of a water conservation program in Las Vegas, homeowners have been paid for converting their grass lawns to gardens planted with plants and flowers with low watering needs. One resident pocketed $1,000 for reducing his lawn by 2,000 sq. ft. And his water bill shrank too!

Prevention is better than cure – if you plant the sort of flowers, shrubs, and vegetables that won't need regular watering, you'll save time.

What to Choose

The following plants are happy to seek out their own water and can cope with drought.

● Trees, shrubs, and climbers (vines) – barberry (*Berberis*), butterfly bush (*Buddleia*), Californian lilac (*Ceanothus*), clematis, cotoneaster, escallonia, heather (*Calluna*), hebe (*Veronica*), holly (*Ilex*), ivy (*Hedera*), juniper, lavender (*Lavandula*), periwinkle (*Vinca*), privet (*Ligustrum*), Scotch broom (*Cytisus*), senecio, sun rose (*Cistus*), weigela, wisteria

● Other flowers (bulbs, perennials, annuals) – alyssum, artemisia, bear's breeches (*Acanthus*), bugle (*Ajuga*), catmint (*Nepeta*), coneflower (*Echinacea*), crane's bill (*Geranium*), helichrysum, iris, marigolds (*Tagetes*), petunia, poppy (*Papaver*), red-hot poker (*Kniphofia*), saxifrage, stonecrop (*Sedum*), spider flower (*Cleome*), tulip.

How to Do it

1. Choose drought-resistant plants. Go for walks in the countryside during a hot spell. Take note of the plants which look healthy despite the lack of water.

2. If a plant's leaves are thick, waxy, hairy, narrow, or silvery, gray, or blue in color, and if the stems are thick, it is likely to be drought-tolerant.

3. Many grasses and lawns can cope with dryness and recover quickly. It's better not to water than to water lightly — the roots will come to the surface and make the plant less drought tolerant.

4. Water in new plants and add a thick layer of mulch (see pp. 14/15) to stop evaporation. Continue watering plants until they are established.

5. Water established plants thoroughly twice a week rather than sprinkling them lightly every day. Water in the morning or the evening for minimum evaporation.

6. Don't plant in pots, baskets, windowboxes — these need more frequent watering; if you do have any of these containers place them in a group.

GARDENING REQUIRES LOTS OF WATER – MOST OF IT IN THE FORM OF PERSPIRATION...
(LOU ERICKSON)
– WHO OBVIOUSLY HADN'T READ THIS BOOK!

Mostly moss

Go Japanese and turn your lawn into an easy-care, evergreen moss garden – then give the lawnmower away, lie back in your deckchair, and meditate!

Posh grass

Before the arrival of the motorized lawnmower the grass was cut by scythemen, and all the grass clippings were swept up by lawn women. Only wealthy people could afford to pay staff to do such inessential work for purely aesthetic reasons and so a closely-cut lawn became a sure sign of belonging to the upper classes.

Mowing a lawn is tedious and hard work. So why not take advantage of the new fashion for Japanese-style moss gardens? A moss lawn will be pleasantly green all year round and soft to the touch. No need to water or mow.

What to Choose

"Accept" the type of moss you already have growing in your lawn. If you're planning a new moss lawn, choose fern moss (*Thuidium*). A low-growing, bright green moss, it thrives in shade, but will tolerate some dappled sunshine.

How to Do it

If you're converting your lawn: stop mowing, stop aerating and all other treatments; dig up grass and allow the moss to take over; kick back and relax.

1. If you're planting a new moss lawn, select the correct location. Most mosses prefer shade, and direct afternoon sun should be avoided. North- or east-facing slopes or wooded areas are best.

2. Free the area of leaves, weeds, and other debris. Gently rake to roughen, then moisten the soil. Plant on a rainy day – press the moss to lie flat on the surface. Water to soak the entire area and press moss onto the soil with a heavy roller.

Aftercare

Moss is super-resilient. It can tolerate severe cold, will recover after periods of drought, does not need mowing, is not generally attacked by pests or diseases, does not need aerating, and is just all-round wonderful!

● Make sure the moss is kept moist at all times for at least three weeks after planting. Water the lawn or spray with a fine mist when it looks dry.

● Brush leaves off the moss with a broom.

● Avoid lots of walking on the moss until the lawn becomes properly established, especially with high-heeled shoes. If you need to walk across it, consider creating a path or laying stepping stones. Keep children and pets off the lawn.

THE GRASS MAY BE GREENER ON THE OTHER SIDE OF THE FENCE, BUT YOU STILL HAVE TO MOW IT...
[ANON]

Get up, stand up!

It's back-breaking work to keep a garden looking great – or is it? If you're not too keen on getting down (in the garden), touch base the lazy way by lifting it to within easy reach.

Sweet and sour

Fill your raised bed with a different type of soil from the rest of your garden, and extend the range of plants you can grow. If your soil is chalk or clay, put acidic or peat-based soil into your bed to grow lime-haters such as rhododendrons, azaleas, or magnolias.

Gardening can be made easier if you raise the flowerbeds off the ground. It'll also create a more private ambience at the same time.

What to Choose

The soil in a raised bed needs to be firmly held in place by a solid edging material.

● Railway sleepers (railroad ties) – solid but very heavy. Build walls up to four sleepers high. Cut with a chainsaw; build in multiples of one or half sleepers. Drill vertical holes through sleepers (ties) and hammer in steel rods to prevent sideways shift

● Logs – use pressure-treated timber. Best for low beds; it may be hard to obtain same-size logs for deeper beds. Kits may be available

● Bricks or concrete blocks – bricks are attractive but more expensive; choose frost-proof bricks and bond with mortar. Concrete blocks can be painted in attractive colors

● Rocks and natural stone – can be laid like bricks or as natural dry stone wall.

How to Do it

1. Decide on the position, size, and shape of the raised bed. A spot in full sun is good. For size, the ideal width is about 1 m (3 ft). Choose any length; several smaller raised beds in a row are more attractive than one very long bed. Raised beds are often rectangular, but you could make it square, L- or T-shaped, or even circular, depending on the material you use. Raise at least 20 cm (8 in) off the ground for good drainage. The easiest working height is about 45–60 cm (18–24 in) high.

2. Clear the ground and level with a rake.

3. If you are using bricks, lay a concrete base or get someone to do this for you.

4. Lay the outside edge. Fill the bed with potting soil (available from garden centers). Do not use garden soil — it is too heavy and does not drain well. You can fill a deep bed to one-third or even half with broken crocks or stones, to reduce expense.

5. Plant your bed — make sure your plants will not grow so high that you cannot reach them.

HARD WORK DOESN'T HARM ANYONE, BUT I DO NOT WANT TO TAKE ANY CHANCES...

[ANON]

23

All natural, dig it?

Go wild in the country – create a beautiful, natural "drift" of flowers in your lawn, killing two birds with one stone: no digging and less mowing, leaving you the time to entertain.

Good luck charms

In Chinese Feng Shui, daffodils spread cheery "chi" or earth energy. If they are flowering in your garden during the time of the Chinese New Year (which is around the end of February), they are said to bring good luck for the next twelve months – so quickly plant some cheery daffodils now.

In a conventional garden most bulbs are dug up in the autumn (fall), stored in a shed, then replanted in the spring. But why not plant your bulbs where they can flourish and multiply as nature intended?

What to Choose

Choose "strong" growers of small to medium height as they will have to compete against the grass.

● Bluebells – English bluebells (*Hyacinthoides nonscriptis*), vigorous; plant on their own

● Crocus – spring- and autumn- (fall-) flowering (Colchicum) are suited; yellow, white, and purple

● Daffodils (*Narcissus*) – the harbinger of spring, this is the classic bulb to naturalize in grass; many varieties flowering at different times

● Grape hyacinths (*Muscari racemosum*) – bright blue flowers in spring

● Snake's head fritillaries (*Fritillaria meleagris*) – white, green, or pink checkered, in late spring

● Snowdrops (*Galanthus*) – the first to flower; many varieties, some have green markings.

How to Do it

1. Choose a site in partial shade, under a tree.

2. Decide on your planting scheme. If your garden is small, plant just one species in a small spot under a tree. If your garden is large, plant different areas up to be in flower during different seasons.

3. The bulbs need space to grow and multiply. Plant them 5–10 cm (2–4 in) deep depending on bulb size, and twice the normal distance from each other (see packet), using a bulb planter. Push the planter into the ground, pull out the grass and soil plug, place bulb in the hole, then replace the plug.

4. Stop mowing one month before flowering.

Aftercare

● Leave plants undisturbed for at least six weeks after flowering. Do not remove the leaves. Pinch out faded daffodils. Leave all other flowers alone.

● Start mowing six weeks after the last flowers are finished at the earliest. Leave the bulbs in the ground for at least 6–7 years.

I WANDERED LONELY AS A CLOUD THAT FLOATS ON HIGH O'ER VALES AND HILLS, WHEN ALL AT ONCE I SAW A CROWD, A HOST, OF GOLDEN DAFFODILS ... ... AND THEN MY HEART WITH PLEASURE FILLS, AND DANCES WITH THE DAFFODILS...

[WILLIAM WORDSWORTH]

25

Shear delight

Don't worry about making the "correct" cut. Save yourself the trouble of chopping anything and everything, and just enjoy the resulting "mess" as a fabulously rich display.

Chainsaw massacre

In one experiment, roses were randomly cut with electric hedge cutters. They flourished at least as well as those that had been pruned with secateurs and obeying all the rules – how close to a bud to cut, at which angle, and so on which just proves that, at times, it pays to break the common rules!

Deadheading is the cutting back of faded blooms to encourage new growth (and to tidy up). But why not leave your plants to set seed and decorate your garden with unusual seedheads?

What to Choose

The following flowers have attractive seedheads that will provide decorative interest in your garden when the flowers are finished.

● Bear's breeches (*Acanthus*) – tall white, brown and mauve; stays unchanged through the seasons

● Bullrush (*Typha*) – waterside grasses, available in taller and smaller varieties, form long, velvety brown, cigar-shaped seedheads

● Chinese lanterns (*Physalis*) – insignificant white flowers develop into orange lantern-shaped flowers

● Honesty (*Lunaria*) – insignificant purple flowers develop into large transparent white disks, revealing seeds inside; often compared to money

- Love-in-the-mist (*Nigella*) – light blue summer blooms fade to large, round, brown seedheads
- Oriental poppy (*Papaver orientalis*) – large red spring flowers, leaving attractive brown seedheads
- Ornamental onion (*Allium*) – spring-flowering bulb, many sizes, mostly mauve, blue, purple flowers.

How to Do it

1. Choose plants that won't require deadheading. Leave and enjoy their attractive seedhead displays.

2. Plant shrub or species roses, which make attractive rosehips after flowering; they're also lower maintenance all round than hybrid tea roses.

3. Plant slow-growing plants so they don't outgrow their allotted space too soon.

Aftercare

Remove seedheads once they become unsightly. An added bonus for the lazy gardener: by leaving the seedheads on the plants you encourage "volunteer" plants – self-seeded flowers will appear the following year, relieving you of even more chores.

MAN WAS MADE FOR BETTER THINGS THAN PRUNING HIS ROSE TREES...

[ANON]

Let others do the hard work while you're sipping your glass of ice-cold Chardonnay — get some wildlife helpers to police your garden and "arrest" any pesky destructive creatures.

Big mouth

Frogs eat insects, worms, spiders, and centipedes. They swallow their food whole and are only limited by the size of their mouth — small frogs are happy gobbling up the odd fruit fly and mosquito larva, but larger frogs may devour entire small mammals such as voles or mice and even small snakes.

By providing the right sort of habitat and sources of food, you will attract birds, frogs, and other wildlife and natural "pest controllers".

What to Choose

● Lacewings, ladybirds (ladybugs), and hoverfly larvae eat aphids. They are attracted by flowering herbs (coriander, dill, fennel, lavender, mint, parsley, thyme), daisies, marigolds (*Tagetes, Calendula*), nasturtiums (*Tropaeolum*), and poppies (*Papaver*)

● Ground beetles and centipedes eat insects and their eggs, slugs, eelworms, cutworms, leather jackets and other larvae. They are attracted to your garden by leafy groundcover

● Birds eat caterpillars, grubs, slugs, and snails. Attract them with seeds, berries; bird tables, baths, nest boxes and hedges for safe nesting

● Build a pond. Ponds are valuable habitats for wildlife, attracting frogs, toads, newts, and dragon-flies to live and breed in them. Don't, however, put fish in — they will eat most of the above.

How to Do it

1. Stop using pesticides, including organic ones. They destroy many of the beneficial insects.

2. Keep your planting varied — include flowers rich in nectar, hedges and shrubs for nesting and shelter; moist, leafy groundcover to provide shade for ground beetles, centipedes, and beneficials that dehydrate easily.

3. Plant "companion plants" to attract beneficial insects near plants that need protection, such as marigolds near tomatoes and cabbages.

4. Plant berry-bearing shrubs and trees and leave seedheads on flowers for birds to feed from.

5. Hang up bird nesting places, out of reach of cats and hidden from view. Set up bird baths and change the water frequently, especially in winter.

6. Don't be too tidy. Some weeds such as thistles provide extra food for wildlife.

7. If you have slug-prone plants such as plantain lilies (*Hosta*), keep them out of damp spots loved by slugs — plant them in a hanging basket instead.

MAKING THE SIMPLE COMPLICATED IS COMMONPLACE; MAKING THE COMPLICATED SIMPLE, AWESOMELY SIMPLE, THAT'S CREATIVITY...
[CHARLES MINGUS]

YEAR ROUND COLOR THE EASY WAY

Chapter Two

HERE'S THE FAST TRACK TO HAVING A FABULOUSLY COLORFUL GARDEN — ALL YEAR ROUND

30

Bring me sunshine...

Suffering from the winter blues? Here's the natural remedy – just take a look at the gorgeously golden blooms and foliage in your winter garden and cheer up instantly.

Mellow yellow

Yellow is the color of sunshine, and if it's your favorite color it means that you are attractive and active, and all round bright, intelligent, and confident. You probably enjoy traveling and you're mentally agile. Fans of yellow are happy balanced people, an inspiration to others – just the sort of person to love your garden.

A large number of trees, shrubs, and flowering plants bring a splash of color to the garden in winter — brightening up cheerless winter days.

What to Choose

Concentrate on warm golden, yellow, bronze, scarlet, and brown colors in your planting scheme:

● Scots pine (*Pinus sylvestris* 'Aurea') – tall conifer, up to 10 m (30 ft) tall and 4 m (12 ft) wide, with blue-green foliage turning golden

● Evergreen honeysuckle (*Lonicera nitida* 'Baggeson's Gold') – evergreen shrub with tiny, lemon-yellow leaves; 2 m (6 ft) tall; 3 m (10 ft) wide

● *Euonymus fortunei* 'Emerald and Gold' – evergreen shrub with green and gold variegated leaves, height and spread up to 1.5 m (5 ft)

● Dogwood (*Cornus alba* 'Sibrica') – loses its leaves but has striking, scarlet-colored young stems; up to 3 m (10 ft) in height and spread

● New Zealand flax (*Phormium tenax* 'Bronze

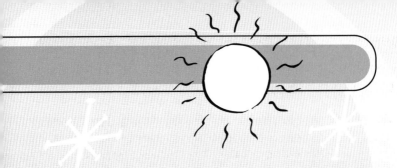

Baby') − large plant with evergreen, deep red-bronze, sword-like leaves, up to 60 cm (2 ft) high; protect in winter.

How to Do it

1. Make sure the area you wish to plant is visible from your windows, or near a path that you drive along in winter so you'll get the full benefit.

2. Plant yellow shrubs as a backdrop, and smaller plants of contrasting red or bronze, in front.

3. In autumn (fall), weed the ground, dig a hole twice the size of the rootball, leaving space for the plant to spread. Dig in well-rotted compost. Place the plant in its hole, refill and firm soil with the heel of your foot. Give each plant a large can of water.

Aftercare

● Cut dogwood back almost to the ground in early spring − the young stems are the most colorful

● Cut both the evergreen honeysuckle and the euonymus to shape them if they become too large or unsightly.

I PREFER WINTER AND FALL, WHEN YOU FEEL THE BONE STRUCTURE IN THE LANDSCAPE... SOMETHING WAITS BENEATH IT − THE WHOLE STORY DOESN'T SHOW...
[ANDREW WYETH]

Very berry nice

Where have all the flowers gone? Don't worry, your garden can look fabulously colorful after the main flowering season by using a simple trick – plan for colorful fruits and berries!

Plant the right sort of shrubs and trees. Colorful berries and juicy fruits will make for delightful autumn (fall) displays of color.

What to Choose

● Firethorn (*Pyracantha*) – evergreen spiny shrub with fragrant white flowers in summer, berries in autumn (fall); 'Navajo' orange-red, 'Waterei' crimson

● Wall-spray cotoneaster (*Cotoneaster horizontalis*) – spreading shrub with white or pink flowers; shiny red berries and red foliage in autumn (fall)

● Barberry (*Berberis z ottawenensis* 'Pirate K') – a spiny shrub with flowers in spring; attractive foliage and fiery orange-red berries in autumn (fall)

● Crab apple (*Malus*) – small, hardy tree with cup-shaped flowers in spring; decorative fruits in autumn (fall); foliage color in some varieties. 'Golden Hornet' has bright yellow fruit, 'John Downie' and 'Sun Rival' have reddish orange fruit.

● Mountain ash, rowan (*Sorbus aucuparia*) – small tree with small, oval leaflets; white flowers in spring and berries in autumn (fall); 'Sheerwater Seedling' orange-red berries, 'Harry Smith' white.

How to Do it

1. Choose the best spot: firethorn grows well against a wall; crab apple is a good specimen plant in the lawn. Barberries and cotoneasters are good background plants.

2. Dig a hole, twice the size of the plant's rootball. Dig in plenty of well-rotted compost. Place plant in its hole so the soil surface is level with the ground.

3. Refill the soil and firm with the heel of your foot. Give one large can of water. Add a thick layer of mulch. Water during dry spells in the first year.

Watchpoint

Wear gloves when planting firethorn or barberry.

Aftercare

Cut out dead, diseased, or overlong branches to keep plants in an attractive, balanced shape.

Endless flowering

Don't get into a sweat planting and replanting all year long – if there are "holes" in your gorgeous flower displays just "plug" them with equally gorgeous plants.

Lily white

A common cure in medieval times for boils, lumps, burns, and snake bites, the white lily was also used as a beauty product. A mixture of lily petals and honey is said to make the skin smooth and wrinkle-free. In ancient Persia it was believed that a woman who washed in lily extract would stay young and beautiful forever.

In midsummer your garden is in glorious bloom and color, but as autumn (fall) draws in everything has finished blossoming and you are left with unsightly gaps. Ensure that your garden will continue to be everyone's envy.

What to Choose

There are countless varieties of lilies, in most colors or color combinations apart from blue, growing very tall 2.5 m (8 ft), medium high 1.2 m (4 ft), or small, just 30 cm (1 ft) high. Here are some of the oldest and finest species to choose:

● Regal lily (*Lilium regale*) – trumpet-shaped, pure white flowers, splashed pink on the outside with golden stamens; up to 1.8 m (6 ft)

● Tiger lily (*Lilium tigrinum*) – golden flowers with brown spots; their petals are bent back, in a shape called Turk's-cap; up to 1.5 m (5 ft)

● Golden-rayed lily (*Lilium auratum*) – bowl-shaped, white flowers with yellow rays and brown spots; growing up to 2.5 m (8 ft).

How to Do it

1. Prepare containers in autumn (fall). Choose two or three 25–30 cm (10–12 in) diameter pots with drainage holes. Fill each one-third with crocks.

2. All the above lilies are stem-rooting: they need to be covered with about 15 cm (6 in) compost so the roots can form on their stems. Plant 3 bulbs per pot, and cover with bulb fiber. Water.

3. As holes appear in your flower beds, move the lily pots into the empty spaces to prolong the flowering display. Each single flower will last about one week, and there will be several more to follow, allowing you to extend the flowering season in the garden by several weeks. Move the pots around to wherever they are most needed.

Aftercare

Pinch out faded lily flowers. Allow the stems to die down naturally after flowering, then cut down to the ground. Replant the bulbs in fresh compost for the next year.

WHERE
FLOWERS
BLOOM SO
DOES HOPE...
[LADY BIRD JOHNSON]

Colorful carpets

Color-coordinate your garden the easy way — with this box
of easy-to-use, stunning tricks to create a superb effect that
will be the envy of the neighborhood.

Naturally colorful

Pebbles, gravel, and stones are found in a range of colors in nature, and are generally sold sorted by color and size — you can find black, yellow, white, and pink pebbles, and some are speckled like ducks' eggs. Pebbles look particularly attractive when wet, which makes them ideal for fountains and streams.

Don't just rely on flowers to give your garden color — polychrome mulches add a delightful background foil and introduce visual interest to any garden, even if it is green-only. They also allow you to create the most astonishing patterns, almost like using a paintbox.

What to Choose

● Colored mulches, made from recycled timber (lumber) and woodchips, are available in a range of colors from red, orange, yellow, green, blue to black

● Preformed lawn edging — buy an attractive aboveground edging material which is anchored in the ground but sits above it, to contain the mulch.

How to Do it

1. Remove any turf, weed, or plants from the area you wish to cover, rake smooth and firm by walking across two planks of wood laid on the ground. Choose your pattern and mark it on the ground using a spray can. Easy designs to use are, for example, a checkerboard of two contrasting colors or a series of concentric circles in rainbow colors.

2. Position the lawn edging. To achieve straight lines, tie a length of string between two stakes. To achieve a curve, lay out your garden hose and follow its curved line. Dig a narrow trench, about 5 cm (2 in) wide and about 13 cm (5 in) deep.

3. Add 2 ½ cm (1 in) sand to the bottom of the trench to create a stable base. Set the edging in the trench. Refill with soil. Firm the ground either side of edging by stamping on it with your feet.

4. Fill the basins you created between your edging strips with different-colored woodchips according to your plan, and your outdoor carpet is ready to be admired and walked on.

Aftercare

When the colors have started to fade in the sunshine, just rake the mulch over so the fresher colors from underneath come to the surface. Replace after about six years.

BLUE IS THE TYPICAL HEAVENLY COLOR. THE ULTIMATE FEELING IT CREATES IS ONE OF REST...
[WASSILY KANDINSKY]

Paint your garden...

Why restrict your gardening to the living things? Just "decorate" the basic framework in whatever color takes your fancy — and treat your garden as a party room.

Healthy colors

It was known even in ancient times that colors have an effect on health. People suffering from respiratory diseases, for example, were advised to spend many hours in gardens richly planted with blue flowers and grass.

Each year, redecorate in the latest fashion. There are plenty of paintable surfaces in the garden, from shed and fences to containers and garden furniture and walls.

What to Choose

Many colors are available for garden use; entire ranges have been created to fit certain themes and styles, including heritage colors, Mediterranean colors, or Shaker styles, and many more.

● Blue is a favorite color for garden decoration. It contrasts well with typical garden greens, yellows, reds. Blue is also the color of tranquility, used in therapy to soothe and relax, and to reduce blood pressure

● Red, the color of dynamism and vitality, passion and sensuality, is rarely used for garden decoration. Many plants flower in red, scarlet, burgundy, pink, and it's hard to find a shade that harmonizes. However, if you plant your garden with green, white, and black plants, red furniture could set a stunning accent. It's the color typical for structures such as pergolas, arches in Japanese- and Chinese-style gardens

● Green is the color of nature itself. It signifies renewal, balance, and stability, and is associated with Venus, the goddess of fertility. It is said to have a calming effect.

How to Do it

1. Choose your colors carefully to blend in well with the overall effect you wish to create in the garden.

2. Choose muted colors for large areas and set accents with small objects. Try out paint effects such as sponging or stenciling on small objects.

3. Prepare the surface you wish to paint, making sure it is clean and dry. Choose a color made for garden use – some contain lead which may be harmful to plants, others won't stand the rain.

4. Give your furniture one coat of paint, leave to dry, then paint again. The paint should last a couple of years at least, but it may fade a little.

COLOR IS A MEANS OF EXERTING A DIRECT INFLUENCE ON THE SOUL. COLOR IS A KEYBOARD, THE EYES, THE HAMMERS, AND THE SOUL IS THE PIANO WITH MANY STRINGS. THE ARTIST IS THE HAND WHICH PLAYS, TOUCHING ONE KEY OR ANOTHER PURPOSEFULLY TO CAUSE VIBRATIONS IN THE SOUL...
[WASSILY KANDINSKY]

Panoramic patio

Why sit in one place when another part of the garden is in glorious color? Just move around to where the action is so you'll always get the best from your garden.

Fiesta

The word "patio" originally comes from Spain where it describes an unroofed inner courtyard. Outside Spain it has come to mean a courtyard or, more often, any seating area adjoining the house. Use your patio for best fun and effect — entertain your friends outdoors and get some of that Spanish holiday feeling.

Over the course of the year, you'll probably find that different parts of your garden look most attractive. You may have a rock garden next to the patio that is in full glory in early spring, but in midsummer a flower bed at the other end of the garden is the most attractive spot.

What to Choose

● Preformed decking is available in large panels that can be slotted into each other. It can be assembled or taken apart without much effort

● Alternatively, produce your own makeshift patio from a series of pallets, painted in your favorite color, and set next to each other for a larger area.

How to Do it

1. Plan for a mobile patio. Think of your garden as a plot divided into the four seasons, and plant each one deliberately to shine in its allotted time of year. Make sure there is enough space near each season to set up your patio.

2. For the spring garden, plant bulbs such as crocus, daffodils, tulips, and rock garden plants like aubrieta, saxifrages, and violas.

3. For the summer garden, plant roses, lupins, land day lilies. Place a water feature here.

4. For the autumn (fall) garden, plant asters, chrysanthemums, and Japanese anemones. Make sure that deciduous trees aren't too close to a pond — it would get covered with dead leaves.

5. For the winter garden, plant New Zealand flax, Christmas roses, bronze bugle, and plants with attractive seedheads or fruit. This area should be near the house, and easily visible from the window.

Aftercare

If you are placing your mobile patio on different areas of lawn, make sure the grass recovers well after you move the patio. Treat it with lawn fertilizer, following manufacturer's instructions, and sow grass seed where the lawn has been damaged or worn away.

THOSE WHO CONTEMPLATE THE BEAUTY OF THE EARTH FIND RESERVES OF STRENGTH THAT WILL ENDURE AS LONG AS LIFE LASTS. THERE IS SOMETHING INFINITELY HEALING IN THE REPEATED REFRAINS OF NATURE — THE ASSURANCE THAT DAWN COMES AFTER NIGHT, AND SPRING AFTER WINTER...

[RACHEL CARSON]

Stripy lawns

The ultimate way to impress your neighbors – create the stripes in your lawn not with the lawnmower and hard graft but with a stunning planting plan.

Waste of time

In most gardens, lawns are the most prominent feature. More money and time is spent on lawns than on any other structure or plant. Yet, apart from ball games and sun bathing they are only used to get from A to B. So it's time for a change, then. Make your lawn a colorful and exciting feature.

Impress your guests, and plant your own multi-colored dream lawn in colorful stripes or patterns by using two or more different-colored grasses.

What to Choose

What we think of as grass may in fact be a grass, a sedge, or a rush. The following varieties are particularly good for color contrast and well suited for small lawn areas.

- *Agrostis canina* 'Silver Needles' – white margins
- *Alopecurus pratensis* 'Aureovariegatus' – golden stripes
- *Carex bergrennii* – brown
- *Festuca amethystina* – blue
- *Holcus mollis* 'Variegatus' – almost white
- *Opiophogon nigrescens* – black.

How to Do it

1. Decide on a pattern. You could, for example, plant a Yin-and-Yang lawn, the Yin side planted with black grass, the Yang side with white grass, and a paved path snaking through, separating the two sides. Obtain your plants from specialist mail order nurseries.

2. Choose an area for your lawn that is in full sun and has reasonable soil. Dig over the ground, and remove any large stones. Lay a path or stepping stones if you need to walk over the lawn.

3. Plant your grasses, about 30 cm (12 in) apart, and water them in.

Aftercare

Cut grasses back as they grow, if necessary, to keep them roughly the same height, using shears or scissors rather than a lawnmower. Cut the entire lawn once a year in spring.

THE MOMENT ONE GIVES CLOSE ATTENTION TO ANYTHING, EVEN A BLADE OF GRASS, IT BECOMES A MYSTERIOUS, AWESOME, INDESCRIBABLY MAGNIFICENT WORLD IN ITSELF...

[HENRY MILLER]

Autumnal welcome

Cloak your door in a profusion of flowers and silky seedheads to make your home and garden a gorgeously attractive and welcoming feature for any visitor.

Silky beard

The wild clematis has evocative country names: Traveler's Joy — its tiny, fragrant blooms cheer the hearts of travelers; Old Man's Beard because of its silver-gray seedhead tassels; Smoking Cane and Shepherd's Delight — in the country shepherds used to smoke clematis stems before tobacco was introduced.

These superb vines create a richly colorful display, lasting from early summer right through to winter — what better way to show off your home to friends and neighbors?

What to Choose

● Clematis 'Jackmanii Superba' — one of the best-liked of all clematis, carrying an impressive display of large deep blue to purple, velvety flowers throughout summer and into autumn (fall)

● Clematis 'Bill MacKenzie' — a vigorous clematis with masses of bright yellow, bell-shaped flowers that gradually open out, revealing a large number of brown stamens; flowers throughout summer are followed by sensuously silky seedhead tassels.

How to Do it

1. Fix a wooden trellis to the wall either side of your door. In autumn (fall), dig a hole either side of the door, about 20 cm (8 in) away from the wall.

Clematis are sold in extra-deep containers — make sure your planting holes are deeper still, so that some of the clematis stem will be covered by soil. Lay a stick across the hole to check the depth.

2. Dig plenty of well-rotted compost into the soil. Place the clematis in their holes, refill the soil, and firm with the heel of your foot. Water the plants.

3. Clematis like to have their roots shaded and their heads in the sun. Place a thick layer of mulch, at least 7.5 cm (3 in), around each clematis stem, or cover the area with large stones. Alternatively, plant some groundcover plants around the clematis, for example a rock rose (*Helianthemum*).

4. As the clematis begin to grow, tie their stems into the trellis. Be careful as you do so — clematis stems are thin and quite brittle, and snap off easily.

Aftercare

In early spring, cut both clematis back hard, almost to the ground — they will grow up to about 3 m (10 ft) again by the following summer and make the best flowers on new growth.

AUTUMN IS A SECOND SPRING WHEN EVERY LEAF'S A FLOWER...
[ALBERT CAMUS]

A tub of hope

Will spring ever come again? Will the days get longer? Will my garden ever re-emerge? Plant a tub of flowers that promise hope, and let their beauty brighten your heart.

Reward of generosity

German legend, says when God created Earth, he asked Frau Holle, the snow-woman, to borrow some color from the flowers. The flowers would not give up their beauty. Frau Holle asked a snowdrop, and to her surprise, it gave up all it had. Frau Holle was delighted and allowed the snowdrop to bloom first every year.

These bulbs are the first to bloom in late winter and early spring. They add a much-needed splash of color to the garden in a drab time of year, and herald the arrival of a new season.

What to Choose

● Snowdrops (*Galanthus nivalis*) – small hardy plants with nodding white flowers, often marked with green, on slender, nodding stems
● Hardy cyclamen (*Cyclamen coum*) – small hardy plants with delicate flowers in colors ranging from soft pink to a deep scarlet red
● Siberian squills (*Scilla siberica*) – small hardy plants with brilliant blue, bluebell-like flowers
● Ivy (*Hedera helix*) – choose a small-leaved, trailing variety, as a green foil for colorful bulbs.

How to Do it

1. In late summer, choose a medium-sized container, about 40 cm (12 in) in diameter, and place it near a window. Fill one-third with

crocks for drainage. Add bulb fiber to fill
two-thirds.

2. Using a trowel, plant three ivies around the
edge of the tub. Firm the soil around them.

3. Now plant your winter bulbs, either all mixed
up, or in groups of the same flowers. Plant each
bulb about three times as deep as it is large.

4. Water the bulbs so they adhere well to the
soil.

Aftercare

● Check your tub occasionally, and water if
there is no rainfall for a couple of weeks

● When the bulbs have faded, plant summer
bedding in the tub, to create an
ongoing display.

THE FLOWERS
OF LATE
WINTER AND
EARLY SPRING
OCCUPY
PLACES IN OUR
HEARTS WELL
OUT OF
PROPORTION
TO THEIR SIZE...
[GERTRUDE S.
WISTER]

Purple haze

Who knew that the color purple could taste this good? Plant a tub close to your kitchen door with herbs that delight both the eye and the tastebuds.

Nice cubes

Harvest mint leaves at their best, chop, and half-fill the compartments in an ice-cube tray with the leaves. Fill the trays with water and freeze. For a Mint Julep, fill a glass with crushed ice, Bourbon, and sugar to taste, then drop in a couple of mint cubes. Freeze 2-3 borage flowers in each cube. Use as garnish.

Our selection of purple and blue herbs makes an attractive feature in its own right, and the darker colors are beautifully set off by the sunshine yellow of the golden marjoram.

What to Choose

● Borage – tall plant with attractive, star-shaped, purple to blue flowerheads in summer; will regrow the following year from self-sown seeds.
Use: leaves and flowers add flavor to drinks, salads, and sandwiches; flowers look very decorative as an edible garnish

● Purple basil – tender plant with dark brownish-purple, almost black, deliciously aromatic leaves. Use: very tasty in tomato sauces and with all sorts of Italian dishes including pasta and pizza

● Sage – low-growing plant with velvety, purple-grayish, aromatic leaves. Use: with veal and pork

● Golden marjoram – low-growing plant with small, bright golden, aromatic leaves. Use: tasty addition to casseroles, soups, and stews.

How to Do it

1. In spring, choose a large tub, about 60 cm (23 in) in diameter, and place it in a sunny position, preferably near the kitchen door. Fill to one-third with crocks or pebbles to aid drainage. Add multi-purpose potting compost, to fill to about two-thirds.

2. With a small trowel, plant one borage plant in the center of the tub. Plant three purple basil around the borage. Finally, plant three marjoram on one side of the tub, three sage on the other. Firm the soil around all the plants with your hands.

3. Give the plants a good soaking, at least two large cans of water for the tub.

Aftercare

● Keep picking and using the aromatic leaves – regular cutting encourages new leaves

● Basil is frost-tender. Using a small garden fork, dig out the basil plant in autumn (fall) and repot it in a small container for the kitchen windowsill, to give you basil leaves throughout the winter.

HOW COULD SUCH SWEET AND WHOLESOME HOURS BE RECKONED BUT WITH HERBS AND FLOWERS?
[ANDREW MARVEL]

51

FABULOUS OUTDOOR LIVING

Chapter Three

GET THE INGREDIENTS THAT HELP YOU GET THE
MOST FROM YOUR GARDEN

Aromatherapy garden

Turn your garden into a healing center. Whether you're down, stressed out, or just lacking in energy – let the aroma of herbs give you an emotional lift.

Nature's Valium

Valerian is not used in cooking. It doesn't contain Valium – the name comes from Latin "valere", being in good health. Its roots relax and induce sleep, allowing the body to self-repair. Valerian preparations are widely used in Europe. During both world wars it helped treat soldiers suffering from shell shock.

Surround yourself with plants whose essential oils have aromatherapeutic qualities. And when you feel in need of some emotional healing, just rub the herbs between your fingers, sniff the aroma, and you'll feel much, much better.

What to Choose

To cheer you up and give you energy:
- Basil – eases tensions and promotes alertness; energizes and protects from infections
- Borage – lifts mood, lowers fever, good for PMS
- Peppermint – refreshing, relief for stomach ache
- Rosemary – anti-depressant, antiseptic, good against headaches; improves intuition

To unwind and relax:
- Lavender – anti-depressant, lifts mood, reduces anxiety; aids digestion and helps with migraines
- Lemon balm – calms the nerves
- Sweet marjoram – relaxing, good for PMS as well as toothache
- Valerian – good against insomnia, calming.

How to Do it

1. In spring, choose a sunny site on well-drained soil, dig over the ground, and remove all weeds.

2. For an energizing herb bed, plant one rosemary and one borage at the back, 90 cm (3 ft) apart. Plant a 20 cm (8 in) pot with two peppermints and plunge in the ground between the tall herbs. Plant 4-5 basils either side, 30 cm (1 ft) apart.

3. For a relaxing herb bed, plant one lavender, one lemon balm, and one valerian at the back, 90 cm (3 ft) apart. Underplant at the front with four or five sweet marjoram plants, set 30 cm (12 in) apart.

4. Water with at least two large cans of water.

Aftercare

Water only during long periods of heat. Keep cutting herbs. In autumn (fall) cut lavender and lemon balm back to just above ground level. Cut valerian back to the ground. Borage and valerian will self-seed, but basil and marjoram need to be replaced every spring, as they won't survive frosts.

SCENTS BRING MEMORIES, AND MANY MEMORIES BRING NOSTALGIC PLEASURE. WE WOULD BE WISE TO PLAN FOR THIS WHEN WE PLANT A GARDEN...
[THALASSA CRUSO]

The outdoor kitchen

Cook and eat outside – the sky is your ceiling, you can smell the fresh air of the garden, and you're surrounded by nature and your family or friends.

Barbie queue

The origins of the barbecue are unknown, and many variant spellings exist. It may have come from Taino Indian barbacoa, for cooking fish over a pit of coals, or from French barbe à queue (from whiskers to tail) or even barbaque (which comes from the Romanian barbeç) meaning roast mutton.

Set up your own permanent outdoor "kitchen" so you can take advantage of warm and light evenings. Barbecued food tastes great and is healthy too, being lower in fat.

What to Choose

● The barbecue – build a permanent brick barbecue if you have the space

● Tables or setting down areas – you need one either side of the barbecue: one for raw food, oil, spices and cooking utensils, the other for cooked food. And you'll need space for the chef's drink!

● Fuel – you'll need about 1.4-1.8 kg (3-4 lbs) charcoal per cooking session (or propane)

● Aromatic smoking and grilling woods – there's a vast choice – ranging form hickory or mesquite wood, to fruit– (apple, cherry, grape, peach, pear, plum, nectarine), nut– (pecan, walnut), and other woods (alder, maple, American and French oak). Available from mail-order companies as pellets, chips, or lumps, each will add its own aroma

- Food – meats, poultry, fish, vegetables, fruit
- Oil – to brush barbecue and food with
- Utensils to turn the food and check if it's done
- Barbecue sauces, salads – and of course drinks.

How to Do it

1. Choose a spot between kitchen and eating area, so you can easily get anything you need from the kitchen, and take what has been cooked to the table. Stay downwind from table and house.

2. Make sure you have fresh herbs nearby so you can easily grab a fistful to add to the charcoal, or to flavor food and drinks.

3. Start cooking the food when 80 per cent of the charcoal has turned white or gray. The BBQ is hot enough if you can hold your hand at cooking height, palm down, for only 2 seconds.

Watchpoint

Once the BBQ is lit, do not leave it unattended, especially if children or pets are around.

AROUND HERE, GRILLIN'S GRILLIN' AND BARBECUE IS, WELL... WHAT DININ' IN HEAVEN'S GOT TO BE ALL ABOUT...

[JANE GARVEY]

57

Dining al fresco

Few things are more enjoyable than sharing a meal with friends outdoors. Chatting over delicious summer food and drink cannot fail to induce happiness and contentment.

Playing footsie

Add a surprise element to your table setting: fill the basin with water, to refresh on a steamy hot summer's day. The table could be set above a jacuzzi – now there's a luxury treat! Fill with white sand for a simpler, but equally sensual treat; it's very pleasurable to play in sand with your bare feet!

Build this stunning Japanese-style dining table, and you'll really impress your guests, making the experience complete.

What to Choose

● Build wooden decking, with all the boards facing in one direction

● Make a recessed area in the decking, to create a lower level for the feet of those sitting around the table. People will sit on the decking, with their feet in this lower "basin". The area should measure at least 1.5 m x 90 cm (5 x 3 ft) or more

● Construct a wooden table, made from the same boards as the decking, but with the boards turned by 90 degrees. The table should overlap the edge of the lowered "basin" by about 5 cm (2 in) all round. By making the table overlap the decking, and by setting the wooden boards at right angles to each other, you create the impression of a "floating" table, suspended from the ceiling without strings and hovering above the floor.

How to Do it

1. Place soft cushions or seating mats around the table on the decking.

2. Add more Japanese elements — place a small group of large stones or rounded pebbles in one corner of the decking; add a bamboo plant in a glazed container; place small lacquered bowls with orchids floating on water onto the table.

LAUGHTER IS BRIGHTEST, IN THE PLACE WHERE THE FOOD IS...
[IRISH PROVERB]

Light up your life

Extend your outdoor party season into the night, and add a touch of magic to your garden with a few well-chosen and well-placed outdoor lights.

Light therapy

Many of us depend on the amount of daylight we get. We feel happier in sunshine in summer, when we're exposed to more light. Garden lighting cannot replace sunshine, but it can make you and your guests happy, allowing you to stay outdoors that little bit longer – or throughout the night!

We're all busy, and many gardens are used more at night than in the daytime. Install effective lighting and you'll make your midnight garden a great success. A well-lit garden looks absolutely fabulous – the ultimate in cool.

What to Choose

Experiment with candles, torches, and electric lights, with colored filters and fiber optics – and turn your garden into a 24-hour party venue.

● Uplighters add drama; use to light a single, striking feature or plant, for example a corkscrew hazel in winter (see pp. 68/69), a tree with attractive bark, or a bamboo; try different positions and watch for the most striking shadow play

● Downlighters, a close imitation of moonlight from above, give your garden perspective; best used to illuminate interesting plants or structures

● Water lighting – hide a light under a bridge to illuminate a pond, or behind a waterfall, creating a shining curtain of water

- Spot lighting – to highlight special features such as statues
- Candles, flares and torches add romance – protect from wind in attractive lanterns and dot around the table, the patio, the entire garden
- Swimming candles are great on a water feature, but make sure they don't disturb the fish
- Solar markers softly illuminate paths.

How to Do it

1. Most outdoor lighting systems are low-voltage. They are fed through a transformer, best sited indoors out of rain, and a protected cable.

2. Cables are usually supplied; if not, use heavy cable and insert it into flexible tubing for extra protection. Bury and mark the position so they will not be cut or dug up accidentally later on.

Watchpoint

Most kits are easy to install, but if you're at all unsure, employ a professional.

LIGHT ALWAYS FOLLOWS THE PATH OF THE BEAUTIFUL…

[ANON]

Water of life

No relaxing or meditative garden, whether designed according to Feng Shui principles or in a western style, is complete without a water feature.

The light of the lily

The lotus, a type of water lily, has always symbolized purity, serenity, and spiritual enlightenment. Its roots in the mud, its stems purified by its growth through water, its petals opening up to sunlight, the lotus flower stands for progress to peace and spiritual enlightenment. Enjoy peace in this garden.

Water will aid contemplation, and feed your senses by allowing you to enjoy moments of calm and quiet. Water lilies bring peace and contemplation. Or add movement and flow to your garden with a bubbling fountain, a babbling brook, or a simple pond.

What to Choose

● In a large, still pond, plant a single water lily to bring great joy. There are numerous varieties in a wide range of gorgeous colors
● For a deep pond — around 1.2 m (4 ft) deep — choose the dramatic scarlet variety 'Esarboucle', which has golden stamens in the center
● For a medium-deep pond — up to 90 cm (3 ft) deep — choose the pink water lily 'James Brydon' or the yellow 'Chromatella'
● For a very shallow pond up to 15 cm (6 in) deep — choose a dwarf water lily such as the dwarf variety 'Helvola', which has soft yellow flowers.

How to Do it

1. Design a natural pond shape, sloping in on one side, to allow easy access for wildlife.

2. Place a single rock on one side of the pond – this miniature mountain will be a counterforce to the water, representing stability and stillness.

3. Use a perforated plastic basket designed to hold aquatic plants. Line with a piece of sacking, place stones in the bottom to weigh it down.

4. Fill the basket with special pond compost, and plant the lily. Finish with a thick layer of gravel to stop the soil floating out into the pond.

5. It's easiest for two people to place the basket: place two long pieces of string under two opposite sides of the basket's rim, then lower the basket slowly into the water, finally removing the string.

Aftercare

Most water lilies grow vigorously. Repot every three years or so, and trim back the roots. Cut off some top growth too and set into a new basket.

IF THERE IS MAGIC ON THE PLANET, IT IS CONTAINED IN THE WATER...
[LOREN EISLEY]

Bop-till-you-drop garden

Invite your friends, and dance barefoot in the garden until the small hours of the morning. Enjoy the intoxicating scent released by an unusually perfumed lawn.

Aperitif on the lawn

Chamomile has a pronounced apple scent — which is why it was named "ground apple" by the Greeks and later manzanilla, or "little apple", by the Spanish. In Spain the herb is still used today to flavor a type of sherry called Manzanilla — just the drink to enjoy as you're ambling across your very own chamomile lawn...

Your guests will be intoxicated with the sounds of music, the wild rhythms of dance, and the sweet scent of a chamomile lawn.

What to Choose

● Lawn chamomile (*Chamaemelum nobile* 'Treneague') — this low-growing, non-flowering, ground-cover herb offers double pleasure: its superb scent is released as you walk — or dance — on it! It looks green like grass, but does not grow taller so no need to mow either! Give an entire lawn or a large area of your garden entirely over to the chamomile lawn, and make this the "dance hall". Alternatively, you could plant a "chamomile seat", a raised bench planted with chamomile, for the dancing crowd to relax.

How to Do it

1. Clear the ground of weeds, roots, and stones as if you were to lay an ordinary lawn. Roll flat with a roller (from a hire shop).

2. Plant lawn chamomile to cover the entire cleared area. The plants should be about 10-15 cm (4-6 in) apart, to allow them to spread.

3. Water the entire area well. Avoid walking on the lawn for a couple of weeks, until the plants have fully settled.

Lawn lottery

Chamomile supposedly attracts money, and gamblers sometimes wash their hands in a chamomile infusion to make sure they'll win. Time to get the roulette wheel out then, as well as the hi-fi system...

Cocktail bar garden

Be the envy of your local bartender — grow your very own cocktail garden, and have a supply of ever-ready flavorings for fabulous cocktails to delight your visitors.

Good herbs

There are many herbs you can grow and add as a flavoring to your drinks. The following is a selection of some of the best.

What to Choose

● Peppermint (*Mentha piperita*) — spreading plant with a sharp, pleasant mint aroma; 30-60 cm (1-2 ft) high; purple flowers and green leaves on short stalks. Good for all-round use in food and drinks such as Mint Julep or Mojito

● Rosemary (*Rosmarinus officinalis*) — woody shrub with waxy, evergreen foliage needles and mauve flowers; 1.2 m (4 ft) high and wide. Good flavoring ingredient for vodka

● Blackthorn (*Prunus spinosa*) — deciduous shrub with pink flowers and blue berries turning black; 6 m (20 ft) high and wide. Good for sloe gin.

How to Do it

1. In autumn (fall), plant rosemary and blackthorn. Space the plants at least 3 m

(10 ft) apart – the juniper could be at the back, next to a fence. Prepare the planting holes, about twice the size of the rootball. Dig in some well-rotted compost and add a handful of bonemeal. Gently tap the plants out of their pots, place in their planting holes and refill the soil. Firm with the heel of your foot and give each plant at least one large can of water.

2. In spring, plant different types of mint, each in their own 15 cm (6 in) terracotta pot with drainage holes, and sink the pots up to their rims into the ground in front of the taller shrubs. Water well.

Aftercare

● Repot the mint once every two or three years – the plants grow vigorously and their roots will soon fill the pots. Cut off a short length of root and replant this in autumn (fall) to grow a new plant for the following spring.
● Keep trimming back rosemary to promote healthy and bushy growth.

A GARDEN MAKES ALL OUR SENSES SWIM WITH PLEASURE...
[WILLIAM LAWSON]

Designer decorations

This stunning hazel makes a "statement", and its unusual stems look great all year round. Light it with a spotlight at night, or take the twigs indoors for a most unusual display.

Great Scot

With its common name, "Harry Lauder's walking stick", this hazel honors Scottish vaudeville singer Harry Lauder, famous at the time of World War I. Many of his best-known tunes are still sung today. His stage prop was a crooked and bent walking stick — which could have been cut straight from a corkscrew hazel like this.

Plant a corkscrew hazel and marvel at its amazingly contorted stems. When much of the garden lies dormant in winter, the leaves will have dropped, revealing the bizarre stems in their full glory. Use spot-lighting to display the shape of the stems to full effect (see pp. 60/61). Cut some for use as an instant flower arranger's display: for a fabulously unusual decoration, just pop them in an attractive vase or other container, without any additional plants or water. You could spray the stems in a color if you prefer, but they look quite stunning on their own. They also lend themselves to hanging seasonal gifts from, such as miniature stocking fillers, or painted Easter eggs.

What to Choose

● Corkscrew hazel (*Corylus avellana* 'Contorta') – a slow-growing shrub, will eventually reach about 6 m (20 ft) in height and spread; twisted and spiraling stems in winter, superb golden catkins in spring, and large, floppy green leaves in summer.

How to Do it

1. In autumn (fall), choose a sunny site and dig a hole twice the size of the rootball. Dig some well-rotted manure compost into the soil.

2. Remove the shrub from its container, tease out the roots. Place in the hole, refill the soil around it, and firm with the heel of your foot. Give one large can of water to settle the plant in.

Aftercare

If the shrub "suckers", that is, if straight stems appear from the base, pull them off. Many plants are grafted onto a different rootstock from what you see on top, designed to give your plant maximum health and vigor. Often, though, the rootstock does not display the same decorative traits, in this case the twisted stems of the corkscrew hazel. Tearing suckers off makes re-growing less likely than cutting them with secateurs.

SHE WHO PLANTS A GARDEN PLANTS HAPPINESS...

[ANON]

Stairway to heaven

Add a certain "je ne sais quoi" to your home and garden, and increase your "joie de vivre" with a simple planting trick from southern France.

Tasty flowers

Cut back scented-leaf geraniums regularly to encourage new leaf growth. Pick the fresh leaves and use them to flavor fruit punches and other drinks, or float a few leaves in a fingerbowl. You could also dry the leaves in a dark, airy room and use them to make unusual teas, pot-pourris, and scented sachets and gifts.

If you've got an outside staircase, you can easily recreate the ambience of a French summer holiday with an entire battery of terracotta pots lining the stairs. If you don't, just use window boxes and baskets to adorn balcony and window with these screamingly red flowers. Alternate the showy crimson blooms with aromatic leaves of geranium to delight eyes, nose, and tastebuds. Geranium essential oil is used in aromatherapy for its anti-depressant, antiseptic, deodorant, and tonic properties among others – as if anyone could be depressed at such a magnificent sight!

What to Choose

● Fire-engine red geranium (Pelargonium zonale) – good scarlet varieties include 'Paul Crampel' and 'Grenadier'– leaves have attractive "zonal" markings

● Scented-leaf geraniums (Pelargonium) – grown for their deliciously scented leaves rather than their blooms; scents range from rose, pine, lemon, spice, peppermint, cinnamon to coconut.

How to Do it

1. In spring, prepare one 20 cm (8 in) terracotta pot for each step. The steps should be in sun or partial shade. Choose pots with drainage holes and cover these with a couple of crocks.

2. Half-fill the pots with potting compost. Plant half the pots with zonal and half with scented-leaf geraniums. Fill with soil and firm with your fingers.

3. Do not water the plants until the soil is almost dry, then thoroughly saturate the soil. Once a week, add a liquid fertilizer with the water. Trim the plants back if stems look spindly.

Aftercare

Towards the end of summer, reduce watering. Over-winter indoors, in a room or greenhouse with temperatures between 10-15°C (40-50°F). Trim back stems nearly to ground; cover with a thick layer of coarse sand to protect from frost. Water very occasionally. In mild, frost-free climates, geraniums may be grown outside all year round.

PERFUMES ARE
THE FEELINGS
OF FLOWERS...
[HEINRICH HEINE]

Chill out in the garden

Once the party is over, and all the guests have gone home, chill out and relax. Shut yourself away from the world and recover in your own private space.

Mayan lifestyle

Columbus first encountered "Hamacs", as they were called, in the West Indies in the late 15th century. The Spanish brought cotton to Mexico, and it was soon the top hammock material. For the Mayan Indians, the hammock is a way of life — they spend almost all their relaxation here, from the cradle right to the grave.

Create a private room, as in Moroccan gardens, to withdraw from the noise — and sleep off your hangover if you need to. This is also a perfect space for some "private" sunbathing...

What to Choose

● A hammock — both ends should be stretched open by a horizontal support. Hammocks that don't have such battens, close themselves around you like a net, making it impossible to get out

● An old blanket and a fold-away mattress — an alternative if you haven't got a hammock, or place the mattress on the blanket underneath, guaranteeing a "soft landing" as you get out

● Washing line and colorful blankets or sheets — choose relaxing, Moroccan-style colors such as terracotta and indigo for best effect

● A side table — this needs to be high enough for you to reach from the hammock; place your refreshments here, mint tea, ice-cold lemonade, or something stronger...

How to Do it

1. Find an area with the minimum amount of noise, away from blaring stereos and road traffic, if you can. You will need some strong tree trunks, or a solid garden fence or house wall, to tie the hammock to.

2. String up the hammock, keeping it low, about 45 cm (1 ½ ft) off the ground, to make it easier to get in and out. You'll also feel more secluded in your oasis. If using a mattress, place an old blanket underneath to protect it.

3. String up the washing line between trees and fence or wall, so the hammock is encircled. Hang colorful sheets or blankets from the line and create a secluded space around your hammock. Then just chill out! You may even wish to spend the night under the stars...

Aftercare

Take anything indoors that cannot stay outside overnight or in the rain e.g. blankets, mattress, sheets.

SO LITTLE TIME, SO LITTLE TO DO...

[OSCAR LEVANT]

THE GOOD LIFE

Chapter Four

GROW YOUR OWN DELICATESSEN, HEALTHY
SALADS, EXOTIC VEG AND JUICY FRUITS

Eat your Reds, Pinks & Yellows

Get the most from your flowers — enjoy their beauteous blooms, inhale their gorgeous scents, feel their delicate texture, then... eat them!

Wonder flower

Pot marigolds are compact miracles — attractive to see and tasty on the plate, they're good companions too, because they lure aphids. Their antiseptic, anti-inflammatory, and antiviral properties have been proven — and they're being investigated for their anticancer action. They make fantastic hand creams too!

Many garden flowers are edible, whether picked fresh, dried, or crystallized, making charming and unusual additions to a fresh salad.

What to Choose

● Cornflowers (*Centaurea cyanus*) — ball-shaped flowers in white, pink, and "cornflower blue," on 60 cm (2 ft) stems. Use flowers as an attractive garnish

● Johnny Jump-ups (*Viola tricolor*) — wild pansy; tiny flowers in purple, yellow, and white. Use flowers in salads, and as garnish

● Sword lily (*Gladiolus byzantinus*) — tall stems with up to 15 flowers. Remove anthers; fill flower cone with dip or mousse

● Pot marigolds (*Calendula officinalis*) — annual; bright yellow flowers. Use flowers and leaves; cut off the white area at the base of the petals which tastes bitter

● Roses (*Rosa*) — all edible; darker flowers taste stronger. Use petals or whole flowers of miniatures; freeze in ice cubes; make into jellies and syrups.

How to Do it

1. In autumn (fall), plant sword lily bulbs at the back of the bed, 13 cm (5 in) deep and apart. Choose one color: blue 'Blue Isle' or scarlet 'Tiger Flame.'
2. Plant a miniature rose of complementary colors, such as the orange-red 'Baby Masquerade.' Dig a hole large enough for the rootball, dig in well-rotted manure, plant the rose. Refill the soil and firm.
3. Thinly sow cornflower, Johnny jump-up, and pot marigold seeds in front. Cover with soil, firm, water.
4. In spring, pull out seedlings so remaining plants stand about 30 cm (12 in) apart.

Watchpoint

● Eat only those flowers you know are edible. Eat only a couple at a time if you're not used to them.
● Don't eat flowers from florists, garden centers, or the side of the road. Don't eat what might have been sprayed with pesticides.
● Remove anthers, pistils, stamens – before eating; wash flowers thoroughly but gently.

I'D RATHER HAVE ROSES ON MY TABLE THAN DIAMONDS ON MY NECK...
[EMMA GOLDMAN]

Heard it on the grapevine...

Decadent afternoons in late-summer sunshine, lounging on comfortable recliners and eating bunches of grapes, fresh from the vine — that's the good life!

Bacchanalia

The Roman god Bacchus was associated with the concept of rebirth after death. He brought the dead back to life, and he also tended grapes — the vines need to be pruned back sharply, lying dormant in winter, to bear fruit in summer. The festival for Bacchus takes place in the spring when the leaves reappear on the vine.

If you follow a few basic rules, grapes can be grown in most areas. They make attractive garden plants, offering shelter, shade, and screening, while bringing a touch of the Mediterranean. Their leaves turn orange, red, and russet in autumn (fall), and you can eat them!

What to Choose

● Which grapes are best for you depends on the climate zone you live in. The cooler your part of the world, the earlier you need them to ripen. There are hundreds of varieties — ask your garden center or nursery for advice about which to choose. They'll start carrying delicious fruit in two years or less.

How to Do it

1. In cool areas, make sure you choose a sheltered spot, on a slope facing south or southwest, to receive maximum sunlight.

2. In autumn (fall), dig a hole, twice the size of the rootball, 30 cm (1 ft) from the wall. If your soil is badly drained, dig in plenty of well-rotted organic material and some grit. Plant the vine, refill the soil and firm with your heel. Give a large can of water.

3. Place a pole in the hole; fix 3 horizontal wires along a wall, 30 cm (1 ft) apart, for side stems. Tie main stem to the pole, side branches to the wires.

4. For the first two years, in the winter, cut main stem back by two-thirds, and side stems to five leaves. In the first year, knock off all fruit — you'll get better fruit in the future if you can resist.

5. In subsequent years, stop the main stem when it has grown high enough, cut side stems back to 5 leaves, cut any small branches growing from side branches back to 1 leaf. Grapes grow on new wood, so the old wood needs to be cut back hard.

6. Give copious amounts of water while it's growing, but stop when first fruits appear.

Aftercare

● If frost is forecast, cover the vine with fleece to protect young buds from dying.

I AM ONCE MORE SEATED UNDER MY OWN VINE AND FIG TREE ... AND HOPE TO SPEND THE REMAINDER OF MY DAYS IN PEACEFUL RETIREMENT, MAKING POLITICAL PURSUITS YIELD TO THE MORE RATIONAL AMUSEMENT OF CULTIVATING THE EARTH...

[GEORGE WASHINGTON]

Fig-leaves

Plant a fig tree for your own Garden of Eden. Figs are velvety to touch and have a unique flavor. You could always use the fig leaves (like Adam and Eve) as you frolic in the garden!

Sour figs

In ancient Greece, the figs grown in Attica were justly famed for being specially luscious. The Atticans were so keen on them, they banned their export during the rule of Solon. The Persian king Xerxes, after his defeat by the Greeks at Salamis, had Attican figs served every day – as a reminder of his failure to conquer their land of origin.

Fig trees are quite hardy and easy to grow. They fruit best when their roots are restricted, so just plant them in a container.

What to Choose

● Green figs – for example 'White Marseilles'
● Brown figs – for example 'Brown Turkey,' 'Brunswick,' 'Negro Largo'.

How to Do it

1. Choose a container, 30–40 cm (12–15 in) in diameter, with drainage holes. In spring, fill the pot with one-third compost. Carefully remove the fig tree from its container, tease out the roots a little, and place on top of the compost. Fill the container with compost all around and firm with your hands.

2. Place the container against a south-facing wall for plenty of sunshine to ripen the fruits. Water the fig every other day during the summer.

3. If you live in a cold area, bring the container into a frost-free greenhouse or conservatory in winter. If a mild frost is predicted, tie some sacking around branches with newly grown embryo fruits. Remove any fruit from the previous summer that has not ripened.

Aftercare

Every two years, repot the fig. Take it out of its pot, cut the roots back by about half, then repot in fresh compost.

FIG TREE...
THE WAY YOU
ALMOST ENTIRELY
OMIT TO FLOWER
AND INTO THE
SEASONABLY-
RESOLUTE FRUIT
UNCELEBRATEDLY
THRUST YOUR
PUREST SECRET.
LIKE THE TUBE OF
A FOUNTAIN,
YOUR BENT
BOUGH DRIVES
THE SAP
DOWNWARDS
AND UP: AND IT
LEAPS FROM ITS
SLEEP, SCARCE
WAKING, INTO THE
JOY OF ITS
SWEETEST
ACHIEVEMENT...
[RAINER MARIE RILKE]

Salad bowl

Grow a healthy, refreshing salad packed with vitamins and minerals in a basket by the back door — all you have to do is pick, dress, and eat!

Salad days

Lettuce first became popular in ancient Rome where vast quantities were consumed at feasts, weddings, and opulent orgies. But the Romans were after more than a cleansing taste — they believed that lettuce could enhance appetite, prevent drunkenness — and was also a powerful aphrodisiac!

Freshly picked crunchy salads are delicious and bursting with healthy vitamins. They're the ideal accompaniment for all sorts of summer outdoor food, from barbecues to picnic fare. Packed with nutrients, they're also low-calorie, so you can eat as much as you like without worrying about your waistline — and in addition, they're surprisingly easy to grow and care for!

What to Choose

● Tomato — choose a dwarf bush variety such as 'Tiny Tim' or 'Small Fry;' these don't grow too tall and have small red fruits, making them best suited for baskets or windowboxes

● Loose-leaf lettuce — these lettuces do not grow a central "heart." The leaves can be picked frequently for use and will regrow; try for example green 'Salad Bowl,' or red 'Lollo Rosso'

● Radish — try a cylindrical variety such as 'French Breakfast' which has pretty oval scarlet fruits ending in a white tip and a good flavor.

How to Do it

1. Choose a large hanging basket, about 30 cm (1 ft) in diameter. Line it with a water-permeable lining material, and place a saucer in the base to hold water. Fill the basket with special hanging basket compost and add a couple of slow-release fertilizer pills.

2. In the center of the basket, plant the tomato. Firm the soil all around with your hand.

3. Around the tomato, sow lettuce seeds on one side and radish seeds on the other. Water well.

4. Keep on watering the basket. Once the salad and radishes start growing, pull out every second plant to give more space to the others.

Aftercare

● Water every day, twice a day during dry periods. Add fertilizer once a week.

● Pick your own salad. The lettuces will carry on growing throughout the summer. You'll have to resow radish seeds once they are finished.

IT'S DIFFICULT TO THINK ANYTHING BUT PLEASANT THOUGHTS WHILE EATING A HOMEGROWN TOMATO...
(LEWIS GRIZZARD)

Club med

Devote space in the garden and the greenhouse to growing Mediterranean vegetables — and bring the health-enhancing taste of the Mediterranean into your kitchen.

Flower power

Courgettes (zucchini) have beautiful, large, funnel-shaped golden flowers, a new one greeting you every day, then developing into a delicious fruit. Fill flowers with a mixture of cream cheese, pine kernels, basil, and a beaten egg, twist together, dip into a thin batter, then fry in oil — delicious!

The Mediterranean diet has long been recognized as one of the healthiest, packed with flavor and nutrients. In addition, the vegetables will make your garden sing with color.

What to Choose

● Courgettes (zucchini) — the immature fruits of marrow (squash); green or yellow; bush varieties are more compact than trailing varieties, but both need a lot of space
● Aubergine (eggplant) — large, glossy, purple fruit; need plenty of sunshine to ripen outdoors
● Peppers (bell peppers) — red, green, or orange fruit; try 'California Wonder' or 'Gipsy'.

How to Do it

1. Sow courgettes (zucchini) in late spring. For two people, sow 3 x 3 seeds, 2 ½ cm (1 in) deep. Leave 5 cm (2 in) apart between seeds and 1.2 m (4 ft) between groups for trailing varieties, 60 cm (2 ft) for bush varieties. Cover in cold areas. When seedlings appear, remove the two weaker ones. Water regularly. When the first fruits appear, mulch around the plants so the fruits do not sit on the soil. The first fruits will be ripe in midsummer.

2. Sow aubergine (eggplant) and (bell) pepper seeds indoors, in trays of seed compost. Place on a sunny windowsill. When seedlings appear, remove weaker ones. Repot stronger ones into their own pots. Start taking the pots outside when it gets milder; leave out overnight, initially with protection, when last frosts have passed. Plant out young plants, about 60 cm (2 ft) apart. Stake stems.

3. Pinch the top off the aubergine (eggplant) stems once a plant is 60 cm (l-2 ft) tall. When four to six fruits have formed, pinch out all side branches and other flowers – the fruits will never ripen if you don't.

Aftercare

Water your vegetable medley regularly, once every day, twice on hot days.

ZUCCHINIS TERRIFIC! LIKE BUNNIES, PROLIFIC!
[ANON]

Vegetarian beauties

Forget about neat rows of vegetables. Plant some flowers in between for a double benefit – they'll keep your plants free from insect attacks, and add a gorgeous splash of color.

Peas in a pod

Finding a single pea in a pod when shelling them is supposed to be a sign of good fortune. Finding nine peas means that you can make a wish once you've thrown one of the nine over your shoulder. Now, whether this is true or just a clever way of keeping you shelling the peas...

Whatever you grow in your vegetable garden, plant some flowers in between, a method known as "companion planting." Good "companions" attract beneficial insects which will devour insects and pests and protect your food crop.

What to Choose

● Zinnias – plant among tomatoes and cauliflower to attract ladybirds (ladybugs)
● Dill – plant among lettuces and carrots to deter carrot fly and snails
● French marigold (*Tagetes*) – plant among cabbages, tomatoes, beans, roses; scent confuses cabbage white butterfly whose caterpillars eat cabbages; attracts hoverfly whose larvae eat aphids; reduces the number of nematodes in soil; deters Mexican bean beetles; good companion for roses
● Marigold (*Calendula*) – plant among tomatoes and asparagus; attracts hoverfly whose larvae eat aphids; deters asparagus beetles, tomato hornworm

● Nasturtium (*Tropaeolum*) – plant among cucumbers, courgettes (zucchini), squash to attract hoverfly, spiders, and ground beetles

● Petunias – plant among beans, potatoes, squash to repel Mexican bean beetle, potato and squash bug

● Poppies (*Papaver*) – attract hoverfly whose larvae eat aphids; keep down weeds

● Sweet alyssum – plant among potatoes and broccoli to attract beneficial wasps

● Wallflower (*Cheiranthus*) – plant among fruit trees and bushes to promote healthy growth.

How to Do it

1. Plant the above flowers between your vegetables, especially choosing the colorful and scented varieties which attract beneficial insects.

2. Don't be fanatical about weeding around your vegetables – weeds, too, help some insects keep pests under control. They do, however, also compete for nutrients in the soil.

MY MAJESTY MADE FOR HIM A GARDEN ANEW IN ORDER TO PRESENT TO HIM VEGETABLES AND ALL BEAUTIFUL FLOWERS...

[OFFERINGS OF THUTMOSE III TO AMON-RA]

87

Go for an abundance of flavor in your garden – pinch or snip a few leaves whenever you like and transform every meal into a gourmet experience.

Kitchen utensils

The woody stems of rosemary are brilliant for use as barbecue skewers – just cut off a short length, about 10-15 cm (4-6 in), strip off the leaves, then thread meat or chicken pieces onto the stem. They will impart a delicious flavor to your food. Alternatively, just throw a few twigs in the fire.

Go potty – grow as many different herbs as you like, all in their separate pots, ready to be used at any time or taken indoors.

What to Choose

● Dill – up to 90 cm (3 ft) high, yellow flowers; use leaves and seeds for fish, pickles, salads, with potatoes and mayonnaise; has medicinal uses

● Fennel – tall plant (1.5 m/5 ft) with feathery leaves; use leaves in salads, fish, and pork dishes; use seeds for baking and herbal tea; aniseed flavor

● Rosemary – up to 1 m (3 ½ ft) high, waxy leaves, purple flowers; use leaves with meat (lamb) and in the bath

● Bay – an evergreen tree with glossy green leaves, growing up to 5 m (16 ft) high if not cut back; use leaves in stocks, soups, stews

● Thyme – small creeping plant, many scents (lemon, orange, pine etc), with small flowers in pink, purple, lilac, mauve, red, white; use in stuffings, sauces, soups, stocks, with poultry and meat.

How to Do it

1. In autumn (fall), plant a 20 cm (8 in) terracotta pot with 2 fennels, and two 50 cm (20 in) pots with 1 rosemary and 1 bay. Cover drainage holes with crocks, add potting compost mixed with a little sand, to fill half the pots. Plant the herbs, fill with compost, firm around the stems. Give each pot a good soaking of water.

2. Plant different varieties of thyme in one large or several small pots. Alternatively, plant in cracks in paving where they'll form a scented carpet.

3. Plant dill in spring, in a 20 cm (8 in) pot. Place all pots in the sun, bay and rosemary at the back.

4. Water herbs only during extended dry spells – most thrive in sunny sites and poor soil.

Aftercare

● Keep cutting leaves to encourage new leaves.
● Snip thyme back to ground level in autumn (fall), using a pair of scissors. Freeze for use in winter.
● Cut bay into shape every autumn (fall).

Sweet basket-case

Just open the window and the mouth-watering fragrance of the juicy, ripe, red fruits will waft into the room. This basket allows you to grow your own dessert all summer.

Love berries

Because of their bright red colors and heart shapes, strawberries were the symbol for Venus, goddess of Love. Be careful whom you share a double strawberry with: according to folklore, it is destined that the two of you will fall in love. Mmm! Is there a variety which always produces double berries?

Strawberries and cream — the essence of lawn tennis and summer. Suspend the basket at mouth-height next to the back door. Irresistible!

What to Choose

● Strawberries — choose so-called perpetual or everbearing strawberries which will continue bearing fruit throughout the summer. Most strawberries are suitable for hanging baskets; good varieties include 'Brighton,' 'Mara des Bois,' and pink-flowered 'Viva Rosa'.

How to Do it

1. Plant in autumn (fall), to give the plant time to establish before fruiting. Rest the hanging basket on a bucket for easier planting. Line with a basket liner and fill with basket compost. Plant 1 or 2 strawberries, with the crowns sitting just above soil level. Give plant a good soaking to settle the soil.

2. Leave plants to grow, but protect it from frosts by wrapping the basket with straw or fleece.

3. As the berries begin to flower and fruit, water them once a day, twice during hot spells. Add a balanced liquid fertilizer once a week.

4. Strawberry plants form "runners" – long, thin stems, at the end of which sits a tiny new plantlet. Snip these off regularly to keep the plant strong.

5. Add a mulch of straw or specially prepared strawberry mats around the stem of the plant, to keep fruits off the soil.

Aftercare

Protect from frosts as described in point 2 above. Once the plant has become "exhausted," and no longer bears good fruit, snip off a couple of plantlets and pot up to get new plants for free.

Watchpoint

Slugs, snails, birds, and squirrels will compete for the harvest. In a basket such as this the fruits are safe from ground-based pests, but watch out for birds and squirrels ripping your basket apart.

AND THE FRUITS WILL OUTDO WHAT THE FLOWERS HAVE PROMISED...

[FRANÇOIS DE MALHERBE]

Table settings

Create a fairy-tale dinner table which magically decorates itself in beautiful colors and keeps on growing more food for you too, all by itself.

A central planter, set into your dinner table, is the perfect container for some beautiful trailing nasturtiums. Not only do they bathe your table in the brilliant colors of summer sunsets, they also impart spice and flavor to your meals.

What to Choose

● Nasturtium (*Tropaeolum majus*) – a trailing plant with trumpet-shaped flowers in a mixture of bright yellow, orange, and scarlet colors; use seeds of the Gleam, Whirlybird, or Jewel series.

How to Do it

1. Build a permanent outdoor table which has a central square or round hole. Insert a planting bowl into this hole; it should be at least 10 cm (4 in) deep. Alternatively, just place such a planter on top of your table.

2. Fill the planter with seed compost. In spring sow nasturtium seeds, spacing the seeds about 7–8 cm (3 in) apart and covering them with a

layer of about ½ cm (¼ in) compost. Water well.
3. As the seedlings appear, remove about three-quarters of them, leaving only the strongest-looking ones in place. Continue watering every day.

Aftercare

● Leave the gorgeous strings of nasturtium to trail over the table, between place settings. Use the flowers as decoration on the plate or as beautiful additions to a salad.
● As the days draw in, the plant will die. Start again with new seed in the following spring, or replant your table-top food basket with another edible delight such as strawberries, herbs like thyme, or tomatoes.

BREAD FEEDS THE BODY INDEED, BUT THE FLOWERS ALSO FEED THE SOUL...
[THE KORAN]

Gorgeous gourds

Surprise your friends with bizarrely shaped autumn (fall) decorations — all grown in your own garden from weird and wonderful fruits that look like alien pods.

Good gourd!

Young loofahs can be eaten, but their spongy insides are the best value. Soak, then wash off skin, seeds, and pulp, leave fruit to dry. What remains is very versatile, used as shock- and heat-absorber in shoes, saddles, helmets, mattresses, door-mats, pot holders. We know them best as great scrubbers to use in the bath.

Summer squashes are very attractive plants, You'll be the talk of the town with such an unusual garden feature, and they can then be used to give you free table decorations, or to pamper yourself in the bath.

What to Choose

Use trailing rather than bush varieties. Mixed seed packets have a variety of shapes, sizes, and colors.

● Bottle gourds — known in ancient times, they are available in an amazing range of shapes, sizes, and colors. May get up to 3 m (10 ft) long or up to 2 m (6 ½ ft) round; colors range from dark green to yellow to very pale; they may be mottled, striped, warty like hedgehogs, or ridged like cucumbers

● Snake gourds — these weird fruits are coiled as a spiral snake, up to 2m (6 ½ ft) long. Can be lengthened while growing by weighing down end

● Loofahs (*Luffa acutangula*) — thick, cigar-shaped fruits, about 60 cm (2ft) long), ripening from green to yellow to brown.

How to Do it

1. Sow seeds indoors in small pots, one large seed per pot, in a heated room, in early spring. Discard weak seedlings. The number you need depends on the size of your structure.

2. Plant out immediately after last frost, in full sun next to a pergola strong enough to carry the weight, 2–3 m (6 ½–10 ft) apart. As they grow, tie into supports until they cling on by themselves.

3. Water regularly, especially during dry weather, and feed once a fortnight with a liquid fertilizer.

4. Loofahs need even more sun, and don't tolerate temperatures below 18°C (65°F). Grow in a heated greenhouse. Soak seeds in water for 24 hours, then put into pots. Pinch out the growing tip when the plant is 1.5–1.8 m (5–6 ft) high.

Aftercare

Leave fruits to ripen on the vines for as long as possible. In the autumn (fall) pick fruits and leave to dry in a box, in a cool, dry place.

THERE IS NO EXCELLENT BEAUTY THAT HATH NOT SOME STRANGENESS IN THE PROPORTION...
[FRANCIS BACON]

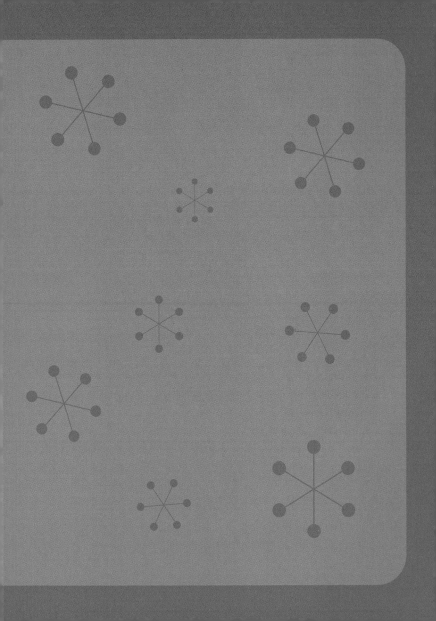

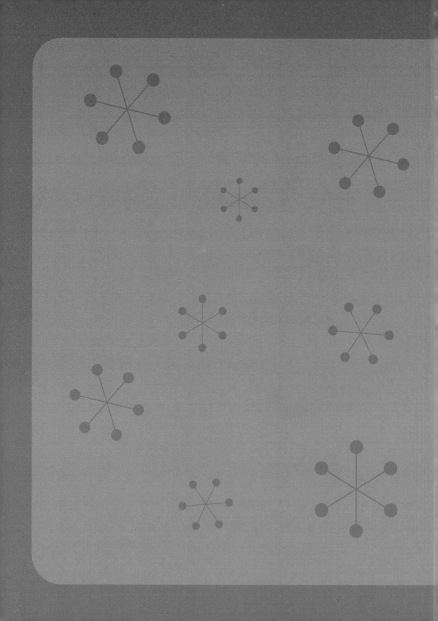